Silly
Rhymes
and
Limericks

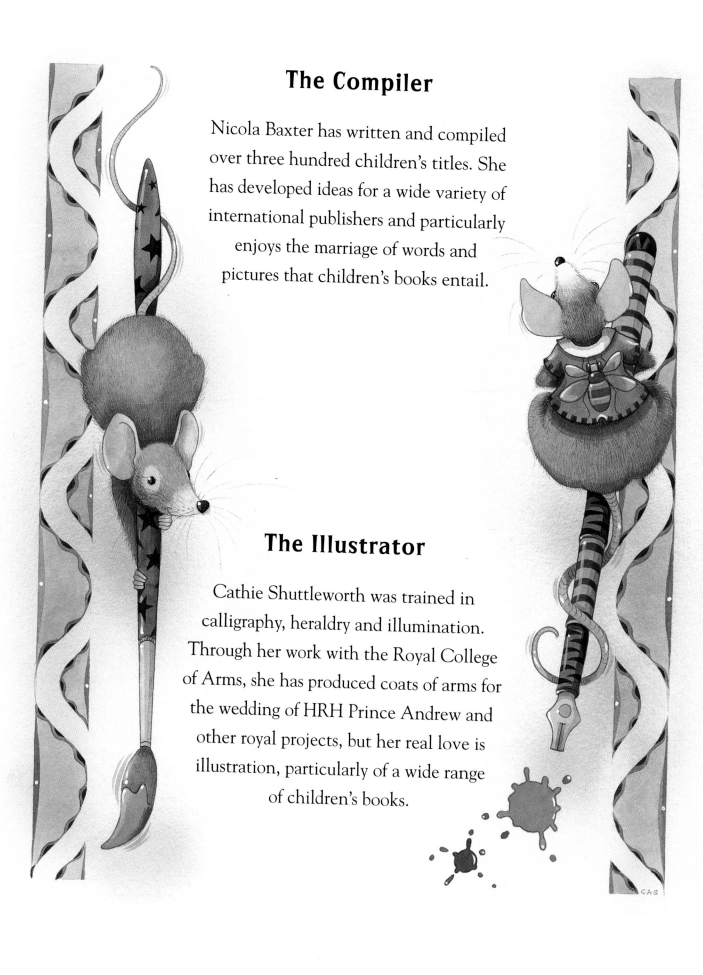

The Compiler

Nicola Baxter has written and compiled over three hundred children's titles. She has developed ideas for a wide variety of international publishers and particularly enjoys the marriage of words and pictures that children's books entail.

The Illustrator

Cathie Shuttleworth was trained in calligraphy, heraldry and illumination. Through her work with the Royal College of Arms, she has produced coats of arms for the wedding of HRH Prince Andrew and other royal projects, but her real love is illustration, particularly of a wide range of children's books.

Silly Rhymes and Limericks

Compiled by Nicola Baxter
Illustrated by Cathie Shuttleworth

This edition is published by Armadillo, an imprint of Anness Publishing Ltd, Blaby Road, Wigston, Leicestershire LE18 4SE; info@anness.com

www.annesspublishing.com

If you like the images in this book and would like to investigate using them for publishing, promotions or advertising, please visit our website www.practicalpictures.com for more information.

Publisher: Joanna Lorenz
Produced by Nicola Baxter
Production Controller: Wendy Lawson

PUBLISHER'S NOTE
The author and publishers have made every effort to ensure that this book is safe for its intended use, and cannot accept any legal responsibility or liability for any harm or injury arising from misuse.

Manufacturer: Anness Publishing Ltd,
Blaby Road, Wigston, Leicestershire LE18 4SE, England
For Product Tracking go to: www.annesspublishing.com/tracking
Batch: 5377-22343-1127

Contents

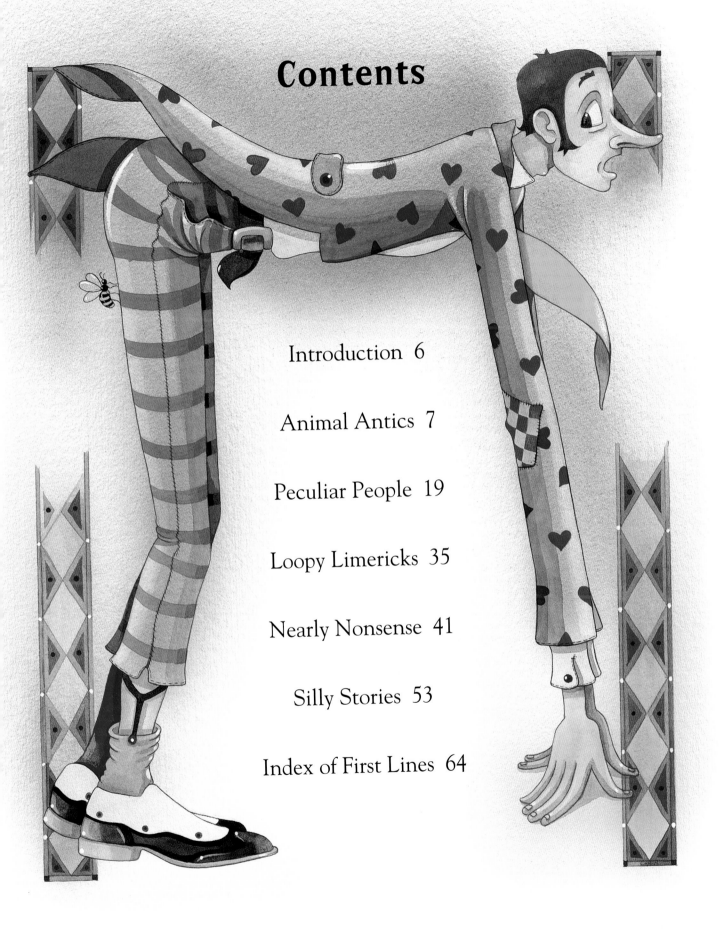

Introduction

Did you know that you have to be pretty clever to write something really silly? Edward Lear was a landscape artist whose paintings were hung in the National Gallery. Lewis Carroll (whose real name was Charles Dodgson) was a lecturer in Mathematics. Today, they are both much more famous for their nonsense verse than for their "real" jobs. Could you be clever enough to write verse even worse than the silly rhymes in this book? Why not try...?

Nicola Baxter

Animal Antics

Elegy on the Death of a Mad Dog

Good people all, of every sort,
Give ear unto my song;
And if you find it wond'rous short,
It cannot hold you long.

In Islington there was a man,
Of whom the world might say,
That still a godly race he ran,
Whene'er he went to pray.

A kind and gentle heart he had,
To comfort friends and foes;
The naked every day he clad,
When he put on his clothes.

And in that town a dog was found,
As many dogs there be,
Both mongrel, puppy, whelp, and hound,
And curs of low degree.

This dog and man at first were friends;
But when a pique began,
The dog, to gain some private ends,
Went mad and bit the man.

Around from all the neighbouring streets
The wond'ring neighbours ran,
And swore the dog had lost its wits,
To bite so good a man.

The wound it seem'd both sore and sad
To every Christian eye;
And while they swore the dog was mad,
They swore the man would die.

But soon a wonder came to light,
That showed the rogues they lied:
The man recover'd of the bite,
The dog it was that died.

Oliver Goldsmith

Turtle Soup

Beautiful Soup, so rich and green,
Waiting in a hot tureen!
Who for such dainties would not stoop?
Soup of the evening, beautiful Soup!
Soup of the evening, beautiful Soup!
   Beaut-ootiful Soo-oop!
   Beaut-ootiful Soo-oop!
Soo-oop of the e-e-evening,
   Beauriful, beautiful Soup!

Beautiful Soup! Who cares for fish,
Game, or any other dish?
Who would not give all else for two
Pennyworth only of beautiful Soup?
Pennyworth only of beautiful Soup?
   Beaut-ootiful Soo-oop!
   Beaut-ootiful Soo-oop!
Soo-oop of the e-e-evening,
   Beautiful, beauti-FUL SOUP!

Lewis Carroll

There was an Old Man with a beard,
Who said, it is just as I feared!
    Two Owls and a Hen,
    Four Larks and a Wren,
Have all built their nests in my beard!

Edward Lear

The Reverend Henry Ward Beecher
Called a hen a most elegant creature
    The hen, pleased with that,
    Laid an egg in his hat, –
And thus did the hen reward Beecher.

Edward Lear

The Mad Hatter's Song

Twinkle, twinkle, little bat!
How I wonder what you're at!
Up above the world you fly,
Like a tea-tray in the sky.
Twinkle, twinkle…

Lewis Carroll

There was an Old Man…

There was an Old Man in a tree,
Who was horribly bored by a Bee;
When they said, "Does it buzz?"
He replied, "Yes, it does!"
"It's a regular brute of a Bee!"

Lewis Carroll

There was an Old Man with a flute,
A sarpint ran into his boot;
But he played day and night,
Till the sarpint took flight,
And avoided that man with a flute.

Lewis Carroll

Calico Pie

Calico Pie,
The little Birds fly
Down to the calico tree,
Their wings were blue,
And they sang "Tilly-loo!"
Till away they flew, –
    And they never came back to me!
        They never came back!
        They never came back!
    They never came back to me!

Calico Jam,
The little Fish swam,
Over the syllabub sea,
He took off his hat,
To the Sole and the Sprat,
And the Willeby-wat, –
    But he never came back to me!
        He never came back!
        He never came back!
    He never came back to me!

Calico Ban,

The little Mice ran,

To be ready in time for tea,

Flippity flup,

They drank it all up,

And danced in the cup, –

But they never came back to me!

They never came back!

They never came back!

They never came back to me!

Calico Drum,

The Grasshoppers come,

The Butterfly, Beetle, and Bee,

Over the ground,

Around and round,

With a hop and a bound, –

And they never came back to me!

They never came back!

They never came back!

They never came back to me!

Edward Lear

Little Birds

Little Birds are dining
Warily and well
Hid in mossy cell:
Hid, I say, by waiters
Gorgeous in their gaiters –
I've a Tale to tell.

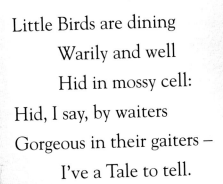

Little Birds are feeding
Justices with jam,
Rich in frizzled ham:
Rich, I say, in oysters –
Haunting shady cloisters –
That is what I am.

Little Birds are teaching
Tigresses to smile,
Innocent of guile:
Smile, I say, not smirkle –
Mouth a semicircle,
That's the proper style!

Little Birds are sleeping
All among the pins,
Where the loser wins:
Where, I say, he sneezes,
When and how he pleases –
So the Tale begins.

Little Birds are writing
　　Interesting books,
　　　To be read by cooks;
　　Read, I say, not roasted –
　　Letterpress, when toasted,
　　　Loses its good looks.

Little Birds are seeking,
　　Hecatombs of haws,
　　　Dressed in snowy gauze:
　　Dressed, I say, in fringes
　　Half-alive with hinges –
　　　Thus they break the laws.

Little Birds are playing
　　Bagpipes on the shore,
　　　Where the tourists snore:
　　"Thanks!" they cry. "'Tis thrilling.
　　Take, oh, take this shilling!
　　　Let us have no more!"

Little Birds are bathing
　　Crocodiles in cream,
　　　Like a happy dream:
　　Like, but not so lasting –
　　Crocodiles, when fasting,
　　　Are not all they seem!

Little Birds are choking
Baronets with bun,
Taught to fire a gun:
Taught, I say, to splinter
Salmon in the winter –
Merely for the fun.

Little Birds are hiding
Crimes in carpet-bags,
Blessed by happy stags:
Blessed, I say, though beaten –
Since our friends are eaten
When the memory flags.

Little Birds are tasting
Gratitude and gold,
Pale with sudden cold;
Pale, I say, and wrinkled –
When the bells have tinkled,
And the Tale is told.

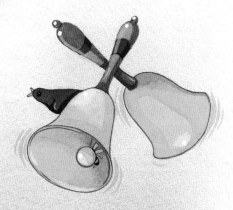

Lewis Carroll

There was an old person of Nice,
Whose associates were usually Geese.
They walked out together,
In all sorts of weather.
That affable person of Nice!

There was an old person of Ealing,
Who was wholly devoid of good feeling;
He drove a small gig,
With three Owls and a Pig,
Which distressed all the people of Ealing.

There was an old person of Ickley,
Who could not abide to ride quickly,
He rode to Karnak,
On a tortoise's back,
That moony old person of Ickley.

Edward Lear

Peculiar People

The White Knight's Song

I'll tell thee everything I can;
  There's little to relate,
I saw an aged aged man,
  A-sitting on a gate.
"Who are you, aged man?" I said.
  "And how is it you live?"
And his answer trickled through my head
  Like water through a sieve.

He said "I look for butterflies
  That sleep among the wheat:
I make them into mutton-pies,
  And sell them in the street.
I sell them unto men," he said,
  "Who sail on stormy seas;
And that's the way I get my bread –
  A trifle, if you please."

But I was thinking of a plan
  To dye one's whiskers green,
And always use so large a fan
  That they could not be seen.
So, having no reply to give
  To what the old man said,
I cried, "Come, tell me how you live!"
  And thumped him on the head.

His accents mild took up the tale:
    He said "I go my ways,
And when I find a mountain-rill,
    I set it in a blaze;
And thence they make a stuff they call
    Rowland's Macassar-Oil –
Yet twopence-halfpenny is all
    They give me for my toil."

But I was thinking of a way
    To feed oneself on batter,
And so go on from day to day
    Getting a little fatter.
I shook him well from side to side,
    Until his face was blue:
"Come, tell me how you live," I cried,
    "And what it is you do!"

He said "I hunt for haddocks' eues
    Among the heather bright,
And work them into waistcoat-buttons
    In the silent night.
And these I do not sell for gold
    Or coin of silvery shine,
But for a copper halfpenny,
    And that will purchase nine.

"I sometimes dig for buttered rolls,
       Or set limed twigs for crabs;
I sometimes search the grassy knolls
       For wheels of Hansom-cabs.
And that's the way" (he gave a wink)
       "By which I get my wealth –
And very gladly will I drink
       Your Honour's noble health."

I heard him then, for I had just
       Completed my design
To keep the Menai bridge from rust
       By boiling it in wine.
I thanked him much for telling me
       The way he got his wealth,
But chiefly for his wish that he
       Might drink my noble health.

And now, if e'er by chance I put
       My fingers into glue,
Or madly squeeze a right-hand foot
       Into a left-hand shoe,
Or if I drop upon my toe
       A very heavy weight,
I weep, for it reminds me so
Of that old man I used to know –

Whose look was mild, whose speech was slow,
Whose hair was whiter than the snow,
Whose face was very like a crow,
With eyes, like cinders, all aglow,
Who seemed distracted with his woe,
Who rocked his body to and fro,
And muttered mumblingly and low,
As if his mouth were full of dough,
Who snorted like a buffalo –
That summer evening long ago
        A-sitting on a gate.

Lewis Carroll

The man in the wilderness asked of me,
How many strawberries grow in the sea?
I answered him as I thought good,
As many red herrings as grow in the wood.

Anonymous

Swans sing before they die – 'twere no bad thing
Should certain persons die before they sing.

Samuel Taylor Coleridge

You beat your pate, and fancy wit will come:
Knock as you please, there's nobody at home.

Alexander Pope

There was an Old Person of Rheims,
Who was troubled with horrible dreams;
So, to keep him awake,
They fed him with cake.
Which amused that Old Person of Rheims.

There was an Old Man of Dundee,
Who frequented the top of a tree;
When disturbed by the crows,
He abruptly arose,
And exclaimed, "I'll return to Dundee."

There was an Old Man of Coblenz,
The length of whose legs was immense;
He went with one prance,
From Turkey to France,
That surprising Old Man of Coblenz.

Edward Lear

Incidents in the Life of my Uncle Arly

O my aged Uncle Arly!
Sitting on a heap of Barley
Thro' the silent hours of night, –
Close beside a leafy thicket: –
On his nose there was a Cricket, –
In his hat a Railway-Ticket; –
(But his shoes were far too tight.)

Long ago, in youth, he squander'd
All his goods away, and wander'd
To the Tiniskoop-hills afar.
There on golden sunsets blazing,
Every evening found him gazing, –
Singing, – "Orb! you're quite amazing!
How I wonder what you are!"

Like the ancient Medes and Persians,
Always by his own exertions
He subsisted on those hills; –
Whiles, – by teaching children spelling, –
Or at times by merely yelling, –
Or at intervals by selling
Propter's Nicodemus Pills.

Later, in his morning rambles
He perceived the moving brambles –
Something square and white disclose; –
'Twas a First-class Railway-Ticket,
But, on stooping down to pick it
Off the ground, – a pea-green Cricket
Settled on my uncle's Nose.

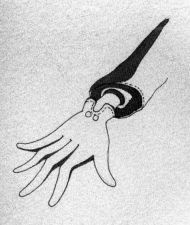

Never – never more, – oh! never,
Did that Cricket leave him ever, –
Dawn or evening, day or night; –
Clinging as a constant treasure, –
Chirping with a cheerious measure, –
Wholly to my uncle's pleasure, –
(Though his shoes were far too tight.)

So for three-and-forty winters,
Till his shoes were worn to splinters,
All those hills he wander'd o'er, –
Sometimes silent; – sometimes yelling; –
Till he came to Borley-Melling,
Near his old ancestral dwelling; –
(But his shoes were far too tight.)

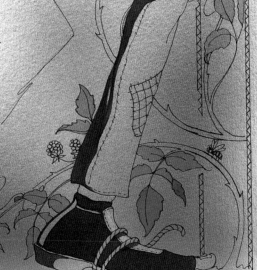

On a little heap of Barley
Died my aged uncle Arly,
And they buried him one night; –
Close beside the leafy thicket; –
There, – his hat and Railway-Ticket; –
There, – his ever-faithful Cricket; –
(But his shoes were far too tight.)

Edward Lear

The Mad Gardener's Song

He thought he saw an Elephant,
    That practised on a fife:
He looked again, and found it was
    A letter from his wife.
"At length I realise," he said,
    "The bitterness of Life!"

He thought he saw a Buffalo
    Upon the chimney-piece:
He looked again, and found it was
    His Sister's Husband's Niece.
"Unless you leave this house," he said,
    "I'll send for the Police!"

He thought he saw a Rattlesnake
    That questioned him in Greek:
He looked again, and found it was
    The Middle of Next Week.
"The only thing I regret," he said,
    "Is that it cannot speak!"

He thought he saw a Banker's Clerk
    Descending from the bus:
He looked again, and found it was
    A Hippopotamus:
"If this should stay to dine," he said,
    "There won't be much for us!"

He thought he saw a Kangaroo
    That worked a coffee-mill:
He looked again, and found it was
    A Vegetable-Pill.
"Were I to swallow this," he said,
    "I should be very ill!"

He thought he saw a Coach-and-Four
    That stood beside his bed:
He looked again, and found it was
    A bear without a Head.
"Poor thing," he said, "poor silly thing!
    It's waiting to be fed!"

He thought he saw an Albatross
　　That fluttered round the lamp:
He looked again, and found it was
　　A Penny-Postage-Stamp.
"You'd best be getting home," he said:
　　"The nights are very damp!"

He thought he saw a Garden-Door
　　That opened with a key:
He looked again, and found it was
　　A Double Rule of Three:
"And all its mystery," he said,
　　"Is clear as day to me!"

He thought he saw an Argument
　　That proved he was the Pope:
He looked again, and found it was
　　A Bar of Mottled Soap.
"A fact so dread," he faintly said,
　　"Extinguishes all hope!"

Lewis Carroll

31

The Akond of Swat

Who, or why, or which, or what, Is the Akond of SWAT?

Is he tall or short, or dark or fair?

Does he sit on a stool or sofa or chair,   or SQUAT,
The Akond of Swat?

Is he wise or foolish, young or old?

Does he drink his soup and his coffee cold,   or HOT,
The Akond of Swat?

Does he sing or whistle, jabber or talk,

And when riding abroad does he gallop or walk,   or TROT,
The Akond of Swat?

Does he wear a turban, a fez or a hat?

Does he sleep on a mattress, a bed or a mat,   or a COT,
The Akond of Swat?

When he writes a copy in round-hand size,

Does he cross his T's and finish his I's   with a DOT,
The Akond of Swat?

Can he write a letter concisely clear,

Without a speck or a smudge or smear   or BLOT,
The Akond of Swat?

Do his people like him extremely well?
Or do they, whenever they can, rebel,
      or PLOT,
    At the Akond of Swat?

If he catches them then, either old or young,
Does he have them chopped in pieces or hung,
      or SHOT,
    The Akond of Swat?

Do his people prig in the lanes or park?
Or even at times, when days are dark,
      GAROTTE?
    O the Akond of Swat?

Does he study the wants of his own dominion?
Or doesn't he care for public opinion
      a JOT,
    The Akond of Swat?

To amuse his mind do his people show him
Pictures, or anyone's last new poem,
      or WHAT,
    For the Akond of Swat?

At night if he suddenly screams and wakes,
Do they bring him only a few small cakes,
      or a LOT,
    For the Akond of Swat?

Does he live on turnips, tea or tripe,
Does he like his shawl to be marked with a stripe,
      or a DOT,
    The Akond of Swat?

Does he like to lie on his back in a boat
Like the lady who lived that isle remote,

SHALLOT,
The Akond of Swat?

Is he quiet, or always making a fuss?
Is his steward a Swiss or a Swede or a Russ,

or a SCOT,
The Akond of Swat?

Does he like to sit by the calm blue wave?
Or to sleep and snore in a dark green cave,

or a GROTT,
The Akond of Swat?

Does he drink small beer from a silver jug?
Or a bowl? or a glass? or a cup? or a mug?

or a POT,
The Akond of Swat?

Does he wear a white tie when he dines with his friends,
And tie it neat in a abow with ends,

or a KNOT,
The Akond of Swat?

Does he like new cream, and hate mince-pies?
When he looks at the sun does he wink his eyes,

or NOT,
The Akond of Swat?

Does he teach his subjects to roast and bake?
Does he sail about on an inland lake,

in a YACHT,
The Akond of Swat?

Some one, or nobody knows I wot
Who or which or why or what

Is The Akond of Swat!

Edward Lear

Loopy
Limericks

There was an old loony of Lyme,
Whose candour was simply sublime;
When they asked, "Are you there?"
"Yes," he said, "but take care,
For I'm never 'all there' at a time."

Anonymous

There was a young lady of Ryde,
Who ate some green apples and died.
The apples fermented
Inside the lamented,
And made cider inside her inside.

Anonymous

There was an old man of Dunoon
Who always ate soup with a fork.
  For he said: "As I eat
  Neither fish, fowl, nor flesh,
I should otherwise finish too quick."

Anonymous

There was an Old Person of Slough,
Who danced at the end of a Bough;
  But they said, "If you sneeze,
  You might damage the trees,
You imprudent Old Person of Slough."

Edward Lear

There was an Old Person in Gray,
Whose feelings were tinged with dismay;
  She purchased two Parrots,
  And fed them with Carrots,
Which pleased that Old Person in Gray.

Edward Lear

37

There was once a young man of Oporta
Who daily got shorter and shorter,
  The reason he said
  Was the hod on his head,
Which was filled with the heaviest mortar.

His sister named Lucy O'Finner,
Grew constantly thinner and thinner,
  The reason was plain,
  She slept out in the rain,
And was never allowed any dinner.

Lewis Carroll

There was an Old Person of Anerly,
Whose conduct was strange and unmannerly;
He rushed down the Strand,
With a Pig in each hand,
But returned in the evening to Anerley.

Edward Lear

There was a Young Lady of Welling,
Whose praise all the world was a telling;
She played on the harp,
And caught several carp,
That accomplished Young Lady of Welling.

Edward Lear

There was a Young Girl of Majorca,
Whose aunt was a very fast walker;
She walked seventy miles,
And leaped fifteen stiles,
Which astonished that Girl of Majorca.

Edward Lear

There was an Old Person of Gretna,
Who rushed down the crater of Etna;
     When they said, "Is it hot?"
     He replied, "No, it's not!"
That mendacious Old Person of Gretna.

Edward Lear

There was an Old Man, on whose nose,
Most birds of the air could repose;
     But they all flew away,
     At the closing of day,
Which relieved that Old Man and his nose.

Edward Lear

Nearly Nonsense

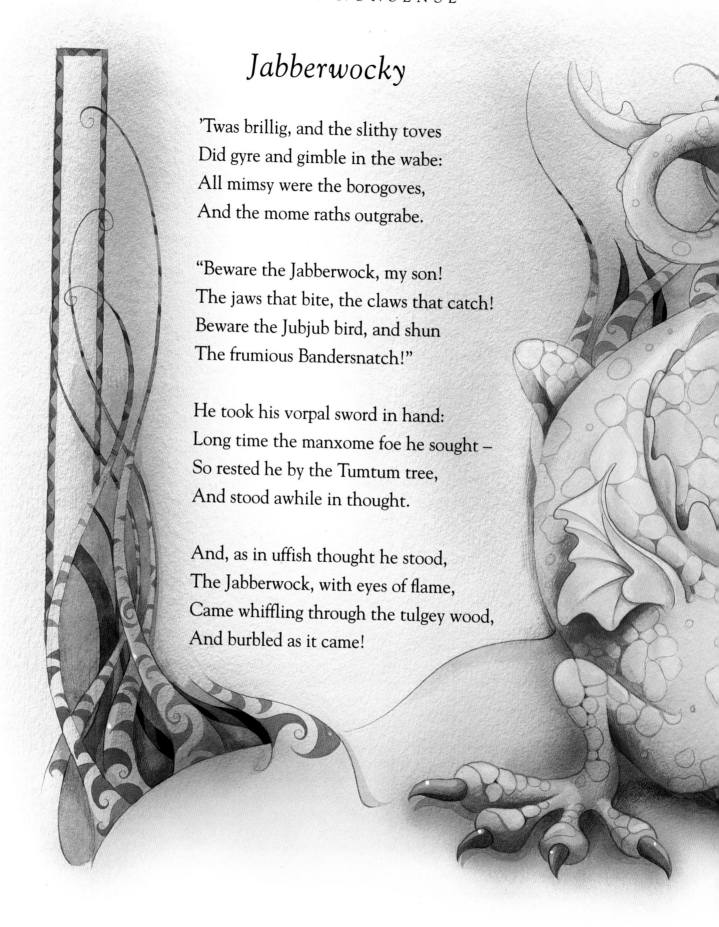

Jabberwocky

'Twas brillig, and the slithy toves
Did gyre and gimble in the wabe:
All mimsy were the borogoves,
And the mome raths outgrabe.

"Beware the Jabberwock, my son!
The jaws that bite, the claws that catch!
Beware the Jubjub bird, and shun
The frumious Bandersnatch!"

He took his vorpal sword in hand:
Long time the manxome foe he sought –
So rested he by the Tumtum tree,
And stood awhile in thought.

And, as in uffish thought he stood,
The Jabberwock, with eyes of flame,
Came whiffling through the tulgey wood,
And burbled as it came!

One, two! One, two! And through and through
The vorpal blade went snicker-snack!
He left it dead, and with its head
He went galumphing back.

"And hast thou slain the Jabberwock?
Come to my arms, my beamish boy!
O frabjous day! Callooh! Callay!"
He chortled in his joy.

'Twas brillig, and the slithy toves
Did gyre and gimble in the wabe:
All mimsy were the borogoves,
And the mome raths outgrabe.

Lewis Carroll

The Great Panjandrum

So she went into the garden
to cut a cabbage-leaf
to make an apple-pie,
and at the same time
a great she-bear, coming down the street,
pops its head into the shop.
What! no soap?
   So he died,
and she very imprudently married the Barber:
and there were present
the Picninnies,
   and the Joblillies,
    and the Garyulies,
and the great Panjandrum himself,
with the little round button at top;
and they all fell to playing the game of catch-as-catch-can,
till the gunpowder ran out at the heels of their boots.

Samuel Foote

A Quadrupedremian Song

He dreamt that he saw the Buffalant,
And the spottified Dromedaraffe,
The blue Camelotamus, lean and gaunt,
And the wild Tigeroceros calf.

The maned Liodillo loudly roared,
And the Peccarbok whistled its whine,
The Chinchayak leapt on the dewy sward,
As it hunted the pale Baboopine.

He dreamt that he met the Crocoghau,
As it swam in the Stagnolent Lake;
But everything that in dreams he saw
Came of eating too freely of cake.

Thomas Hood

The Duck and the Kangaroo

Said the Duck to the Kangaroo,
    "Good gracious! how you hop!
Over the fields and the water too,
    As if you never would stop!
My life is a bore in this nasty pond,
And I long to go out in the world beyond!
    I wish I could hop like you!"
    Said the Duck to the Kangaroo.

"Please give me a ride on your back!"
    Said the Duck to the Kangaroo.
"I would sit quite still, and say nothing but 'Quack,'
    The whole of the long day through!
And we'd go to the Dee, and the Jelly Bo Lee,
Over the land, and over the sea; –
    Please take me a ride! O do!"
    Said the Duck to the Kangaroo.

Said the Kangaroo to the Duck,
    "This requires some little reflection;
Perhaps on the whole it might bring me luck,
    And there seems but one objection,
Which is, if you'll let me speak so bold,
Your feet are unpleasantly wet and cold,
And would probably give me the roo –
    Matiz!" said the Kangaroo.

Said the Duck, "As I sat on the rocks,
    I have thought over that completely,
And I bought four pairs of worsted socks
    Which fit my web-feet neatly.
And to keep out the cold I've bought a cloak,
And every day a cigar I'll smoke,
    All to follow my own dear true
    Love of a Kangaroo!"

Said the Kangaroo, "I'm ready!
    All in the moonlight pale;
But to balance me well, dear Duck, sit steady!
    And quite at the end of my tail!"
So away they went with a hop and a bound,
And they hopped the whole world three times round;
    And who so happy, – O who,
    As the Duck and the Kangaroo?

Edward Lear

To Marie

When the breeze from the bluebottle's blustering blim
Twirls the toads in a tooramaloo,
And the whiskery whine of the wheedlesome whim
Drowns the roll of the rattatattoo,
Then I dream in the shade of the shally-g-shee,
And the voice of the bally-molay
Brings the smell of the pale poppy-cod's blummered blee
From the willy-wad over the way.

Ah, the shuddering shoe and the blinketty-blanks
When the punglung falls from the bough
In the blast of a hurricane's hicketty-hanks
O'er the hills of the hocketty-how!
Give the rigamarole to the clangery-whang,
If they care for such fiddlededee;
But the thingumbob kiss of the whangery-bang
Keeps the higgledy-piggle for me.

Anonymous

L'Envoi

It is pilly-po-doddle and aligobung
When the lollypup covers the ground,
Yet the poldiddle perishes plunkety-pung
When the heart jimny-coggles around.
If the soul cannot snoop at the gigglesome cart
Seeking surcease in gluggety-glug,
It is useless to say to the pulsating heart,
"Yankee-doodle ker-chuggety-chug!"

Anonymous

I Saw a Peacock

I saw a peacock with a fiery tail
I saw a blazing comet pour down hail
I saw a cloud all wrapt with ivy round
I saw a lofty oak creep on the ground
I saw a beetle swallow up a whale
I saw a foaming sea brimful of ale
I saw a pewter cup sixteen feet deep
I saw a well full of men's tears that weep
I saw wet eyes in flames of living fire
I saw a house as high as the moon and higher
I saw the glorious sun at deep midnight
I saw the man who saw this wondrous sight.

I saw a fishpond all on fire
I saw a houe bow to a squire
I saw a parson twelve feet high
I saw a cottage near the sky
I saw a balloon made of lead
I saw a coffin drop down dead
I saw a sparrow run a race
I saw two horses making lace
I saw a girl just like a cat
I saw a kitten wear a hat
I saw a man who saw these too,
And say, though strange, they all are true.

Anonymous

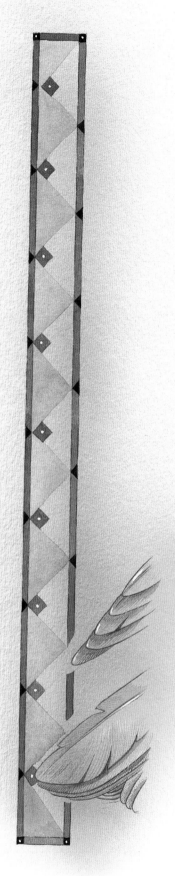

Muddled Metaphors

Oh, ever thus from childhood's hour
I've seen my fondest hopes recede!
I never loved a tree or flower
That didn't trump its partner's lead.

I never nursed a dear gazelle,
To glad me with its dappled hide,
But when it came to know me well
It fell upon the buttered side.

I never taught a cockatoo
To whistle comic songs profound,
But just when "Jolly Dogs" it knew
It failed for ninepence in the pound.

I never reared a walrus cub
In my aquarium to plunge,
But, when it learnt to love its tub,
It placidly threw up the sponge.

I never strove a metaphor
To every bosom home to bring,
But – just as it had reached the door –
It went and cut a pigeon's wing.

Thomas Hood

Silly Stories

Sally Simpkin's Lament or John Jones's Kit-Cat-astrophe

"Oh! what is that comes gliding in,
And quite in middling haste?
It is the picture of my Jones,
And painted to the waist.

"It is not painted to the life,
For where's the trowsers blue?
Oh Jones, my dear! – Oh dear! my Jones,
What is become of you?"

"Oh! Sally dear, it is too true, –
The half that you remark
Is come to say my other half
Is bit off by a shark!

"Oh! Sally, sharks do things by halves,
Yet most completely do!
A bite in one place seems enough,
But I've been bit in two.

"You know I once was all your own,
But now a shark must share!
But let that pass – for now to you
I'm neither here nor there.

"Alas! death has a strange divorce
Effected in the sea,
It has divided me from you,
And even me from me!

"Don't fear my ghost will walk 'o nights
To haunt as people say;
My ghost can't walk, for, oh! my legs
Are many leagues away!

"Lord! think when I am swimming round,
And looking where the boat is,
A shark just snaps away a half,
Without 'a quarter's notice'.

"One half is here, the other half
Is near Columbia placed;
Oh! Sally, I have got the whole
Atlantic for my waist.

"But now, adieu – a long adieu!
I've solved death's awful riddle,
And would say more, but I am doomed
To break off in the middle."

Thomas Hood

The Walrus and the Carpenter

The sun was shining on the sea
Shining with all his might:
He did his very best to make
The billows smooth and bright –
And this was odd, because it was
The middle of the night.

The moon was shining sulkily,
Because she thought the sun
Had got no business to be there
After the day was done –
"It's very rude of him," she said,
"To come and spoil the fun!"

The sea was wet as wet could be,
The sands were dry as dry.
You could not see a cloud, because
No cloud was in the sky:
No birds were flying overhead –
There were no birds to fly.

The Walrus and the Carpenter
Were walking close at hand;
They wept like anything to see
Such quantities of sand:
"If this were only cleared away,"
They said, "it would be grand!"

"If seven maids with seven mops
Swept it for half a year,
Do you suppose," the Walrus said,
"That they could get it clear?"
"I doubt it," said the Carpenter,
And shed a bitter tear.

"O Oysters, come and walk with us!"
The Walrus did beseech.
"A pleasant walk, a pleasant talk,
Along the briny beach:
We cannot do with more than four,
To give a hand to each."

The eldest Oyster looked at him,
But never a word he said:
The eldest Oyster winked his eye,
And shook his heavy head –
Meaning to say he did not choose
To leave the oyster-bed.

But four young Oysters hurried up,
All eager for the treat:
Their coats were brushed, their faces washed,
Their shoes were clean and neat –
And this was odd, because, you know,
They hadn't any feet.

Four other Oysters followed them,
And yet another four;
And thick and fast they came at last,
And more, and more, and more –
All hopping through the frothy waves,
And scrambling to the shore.

The Walrus and the Carpenter
Walked on a mile or so.
And then they rested on a rock
Conveniently low:
And all the little Oysters stood
And waited in a row.

"The time has come," the Walrus said,
"To talk of many things:
Of shoes – sand ships – and sealing-wax –
Of cabbages – and kings –
And why the sea is boiling hot –
And whether pigs have wings."

"But wait a bit," the Oysters cried,
"Before we have our chat;
For some of us are out of breath,
And all of us are fat!"
"No hurry!" said the Carpenter.
They thanked him much for that.

"A loaf of bread," the Walrus said,
"Is what we chiefly need:
Pepper and vinegar besides
Are very good indeed –
Now if you're ready, Oysters dear,
We can begin to feed."

"But not on us!" the Oysters cried,
Turning a little blue.
"After such kindness, that would be
A dismal thing to do!"
"The night is fine," the Walrus said,
"Do you admire the view?"

"It was so kind of you to come!
And you are very nice!"
The Carpenter said nothing but
"Cut us another slice:
I wish you were not quite so deaf –
I've had to ask you twice!"

"It seems a shame," the Walrus said,
"To play them such a trick,
After we've brought them out so far,
And made them trot so quick!"
The Carpenter said nothing but
"The butter's spread too thick!"

"I weep for you," the Walrus said:
"I deeply sympathize."
With sobs and tears he sorted out
Those of the largest size,
Holding his pocket-handkerchief
Before his streaming eyes.

"O Oysters," said the Carpenter,
"You've had a pleasant run!
Shall we be trotting home again?"
But answer came there none –
And this was scarcely odd, because
They'd eaten every one.

Lewis Carroll

Simple Simon

Simple Simon met a pieman
Going to the fair;
Says Simple Simon to the pieman,
Let me taste your ware.

Says the pieman to Simple Simon,
Show me first your penny;
Says Simple Simon to the pieman,
Indeed I have not any.

Simple Simon went a-fishing,
For to catch a whale;
All the water he had got
Was in his mother's pail.

Simple Simon went a-hunting,
For to catch a hare;
He rode a goat about the streets,
But couldn't find one there.

He went to catch a dickey bird,
And thought he could not fail,
Because he'd got a little salt
To put upon its tail.

He went to shoot a wild duck,
But wild duck flew away;
Says Simon, I can't hit him,
Because he will not stay.

He went to ride a spotted cow,
That had a little calf;
She threw him down upon the ground,
Which made the people laugh.

Once Simon made a great snowball,
And brought it in to roast;
He laid it down before the fire,
And soon the ball was lost.

He went to try if cherries ripe
Did grow upon a thistle;
He pricked his finger very much
Which made poor Simon whistle.

He went for water in a sieve,
But soon it all ran through;
And now poor Simple Simon
Bids you all adieu.

Anonymous

Index of First Lines